The Marvellous Mind of Fergus Frank:

The Boy Who Didn't Want to Go to School

Author: Jamie Souter

Illustrated by: Ari and Alex Paul

Author's Biography:

Jamie Souter, the author of "The Marvellous Mind of Fergus Frank: The Boy Who Didn't Want to Go to School," is a talented storyteller who captivates young readers. Inspired by everyday magic, Jamie weaves enchanting tales that touch hearts. Through relatable characters, Jamie explores bravery, friendship, and personal growth. Jamie's engaging style and memorable characters resonate with both young and adult readers, fostering a love for reading, empathy, and curiosity. As an emerging author, Jamie continues to create meaningful stories, inviting readers on transformative journeys.

Dedication:

This book is dedicated to all the young hearts who have ever faced fear and adversity. May you find courage within yourselves and discover the remarkable powers of your own minds. May this story remind you that kindness, wit, and understanding have the power to transform not only your own experiences but also others around you.

Acknowledgement:

I would like to express my heartfelt gratitude to all those who have contributed to the creation of "The Marvellous Mind of Fergus Frank: The Boy Who Didn't Want to Go to School." To my brother and family, thank you for the extensive critique as well as encouragement. To Ari and Alex the talented illustrators, your captivating artwork breathes life into the story. To all the readers, young and old, I sincerely hope you find joy, inspiration, and a sense of empowerment within the pages of this book.

In the town of
Higgledy-Piggledy,
near the windy
riverbank,

Lived a young and timid
lad known
to all as
Fergus Frank.

Fergus was a
kindhearted boy, but his
days were filled with
strife,

For within the school's
playground, he was fearful
for his very life.

One morning Fergus
wept aloud, not wanting
to
face the day,

"Mummy, I can't go to
school, please just let me
hide away!"

His mother, with a tender voice,

inquired about his plight,

"What's wrong, my dearest Fergus?

Why are you so full of fright?"

He said, "There is a bully,

Billy McBoot, he torments

me each day,

In the playground, he kicks me,

he takes my snacks away!

His father, a wise and

gentle soul,

looked over and softly said,

"Fergus, my lad, a

superpower

lies within your head.

Your mind is quick;

you can outsmart him; you'll see,

Just find his hidden secret, his

weakness - that's the key.

Most bullies are quite silly

and often insecure.

Be clever, make him laugh,

say something immature."

So Fergus went to school that day

determined to be brave,

He marched into the classroom

and gave McBoot a wave.

He said, "Billy McBoot,

come over here.

I have a silly song,

It's truly quite infectious,

you'll be humming all day long.

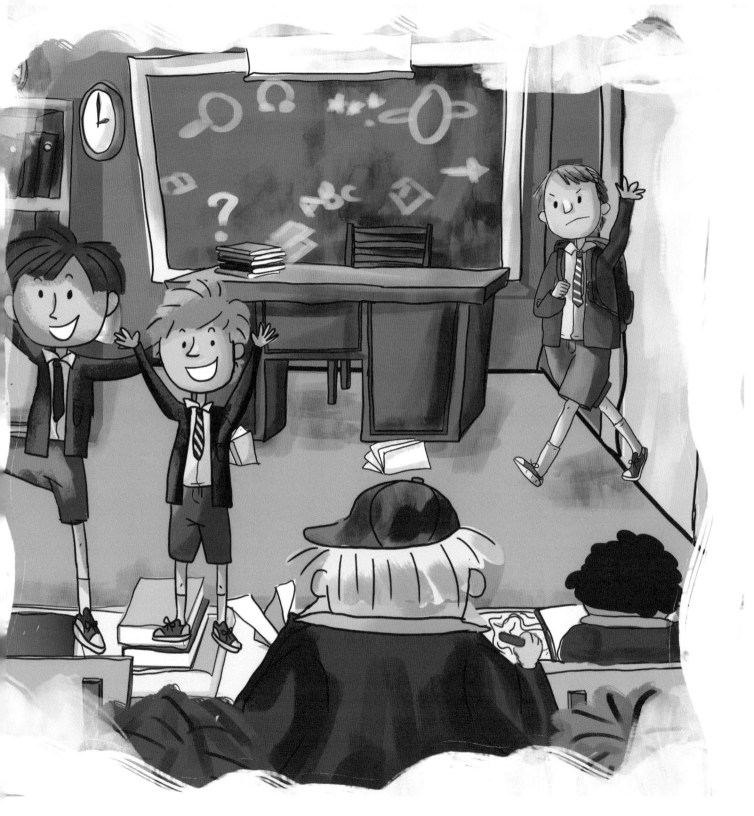

He took in a breath and began to croon the tune, So very catchy, other children filled the room:

"Beans, beans, they're good for you McBoot,
The more you eat, the more you toot.
The more you toot, the better you'll feel,
So, eat beans McBoot, for every meal!

Oh Beans, beans, they're such a hoot,
The more you eat, the more you toot.
The more you toot, the better you feel,
So lift a leg McBoot and let them squeal!"

Billy McBoot blinked in surprise,

then he started to chuckle,

His laughter grew and grew until his

knees began to buckle.

Fergus couldn't believe his luck as

he watched the bully's grin,

He had discovered the secret that,

with laughter, he could win.

But as the days went by,

Billy McBoot's old ways returned,

As being nice to everyone,

he was still to learn.

Now he targeted little Jenny,

taunting her with words so cruel,

Each time she walked past him,

he'd point and ridicule.

Fergus, fuelled by newfound
bravery, knew just what to do,
This bully has to change,
his actions are mean
and untrue.

With a brave face, he hollered,

"Hey, Billy McBoot, come near!

I've jokes to share. They're rib ticklers,

likely to bring a cheer!"

Billy McBoot shifted his gaze,

his interest now stirred,

He left young Jenny alone,

to Fergus' side he whirred.

"Why did the cow venture

to the vast expanse of space?

To see the moooon, of course,

and put a smile upon your face!"

McBoot's laughter remained stifled.

He merely gave a huff,

So Fergus tried once more,

with other funny stuff...

"Why did the ketchup blush, my friend?
I'll share the reason why,
It saw the salad dressing and
suddenly felt shy!"
McBoot smiled for a second,
his face starting to shine,
As others gathered closer
to hear another line.
"If I asked the name of cheese
that isn't yours, what would you say?"
"Nacho cheese, of course!"
Fergus said without delay.

This time the laughter bubbles,

and Billy's eyes gleam,

As Fergus' final joke had

worked just like a dream.

From that day on, Fergus realized

that his mind held the key,

To protect not just himself

but others from the

bully's tyranny.

One sunny afternoon,
Fergus and Jenny
stumbled upon a sight,
Billy McBoot was crying;
his brothers had hurt him in a fight.

Fergus whispered to Jenny,
"He's sad. He needs some friends,
Perhaps we should help him
try to make amends."

Together, they approached
the lonely bully with a plan,
To include him in their games
and add him to their clan.

"Hey, Billy McBoot,"
Fergus called,

"Would you like to play?

We're about to start a game,

and we'd love for you

to stay!"

The bully's eyes widened,

surprise etched upon his face,

For people rarely showed him

kindness

or a warm

embrace.

He nodded hesitantly, joining

Fergus and Jenny's crew,

Playing,

laughing,

and having fun,

as he'd never known to do.

Though he seemed cruel at first,

Billy had a secret to share,

He was often scared at home

but hid this with great care.

He told them of his nasty brothers,

who made him fear the night,

And that by acting tough,

he kept his troubles out of sight.

With Billy's consent,
Fergus and Jenny

sought the teachers' aid,

And with some intervention,

Billy's troubles began

to fade.

Once again, Fergus' clever mind had proven
to be the key,
In solving the problem,
and this time, setting
Billy McBoot free.

By supporting Billy McBoot,

they'd helped him

change his ways,

And now, the playground

was a haven where all

could enjoy their days.

Moral of the story:

"The Marvellous Mind of Fergus Frank: The Boy Who Didn't Want to Go to School" carries a significant moral message for readers of all ages. It reminds us that within each of us lies the power to overcome challenges and stand up against adversity. It teaches us the importance of understanding and empathy, showing us that kindness and compassion can turn foes into friends. The story encourages us to embrace our unique strengths, use our minds creatively, and find peaceful solutions to conflicts. Ultimately, it highlights the transformative power of laughter, friendship, and the indomitable spirit of the human mind.

Printed in Great Britain
by Amazon

31757382R00032